THE AGE OF APOSTOLIC APOSTLESHIP SERIES

Developments
and
Provision

PART 4

On Behalf of

Connecting for Excellence
International Apostolic Network
CHURCHES AND MINISTRIES IN ASSOCIATION

BY DR. ALAN PATEMAN

BY DR. JENNIFER PATEMAN

AVAILABLE FROM APMI PUBLICATIONS, AMAZON.COM AND OTHER RETAIL OUTLETS

THE AGE OF APOSTOLIC APOSTLESHIP SERIES

Developments
and
Provision

PART 4

DR. ALAN PATEMAN

BOOK TITLE: Developments and Provision
(The Age of Apostolic Apostleship Series) Part Four

WRITTEN BY Dr. ALAN PATEMAN
ISBN: 978-1-909132-62-7
eBook ISBN: 978-1-909132-63-4

Published By:
APMI Publications
In Partnership with Truth for the Journey Books 22
Email: publications@alanpateman.com
www.AlanPatemanMinistries.com

Acknowledgements:
Author/Design/Senior Editor/Publisher: Apostle Dr. Alan Pateman
Editing/Proofreading/Research: Dr. Jennifer Pateman
Computer Administration/Office Manager: Dr. Dorothea Struhlik
Cover Image Credit: www.PosterMyWall.com

Unless otherwise indicated, all scriptural quotations are from the HOLY BIBLE, NEW INTERNATIONAL VERSION ®. NIV ®. Copyright © 1973, 1978, 1984 by the International Bible Society. Used by permission of Zondervan Publishing House. All rights reserved.

*Where scriptures appear with special emphasis (**in bold,** italic or <u>underlined</u>) we have edited them ourselves in order to bring focused attention within the context of this subject being taught.*

❖

My Prayer

My prayer for all of you, who read this book, is that God blesses you and that He will enlarge your territory. Taken from the following scripture is this wonderful prayer, which I recommend you confess and pray over your Church, Ministry & Family etc. Cry out as Jabez did and see God grant your request!

"Oh, that you would bless me and enlarge my territory! Let your hand be with me, and keep me from harm so that I will be free from pain." And God granted his request.
(1 Chronicles 4:10)

❖

Dedication

I dedicate and submit this book **"Developments and Provision,"** part four of "The Age of Apostolic Apostleship" series to God the Author and Perfecter of all things and pray that the anointing of His Holy Spirit will rest upon all those who are in relationship with this network.

❖

Table of Contents

❖

Personal Invitation

Dear Friend, Greetings in the Name of Jesus, He is building His Apostolic Church, restoring righteousness and *spiritual government,* which no gate of hell can prevail! *Amen.*

Please receive this book as a personal invitation to become part of the "Connecting for Excellence Apostolic Network."

Within these pages I have the privilege of sharing with you and introducing to you the work of this ministry and **the vision** behind it. I hope you find it an exciting discovery! And become a part or member of this network of association, *(or affiliation)* or just support, then don't delay we would love to hear from you.

You may also ask yourself the question, Do I have the training needed? My prayer is that *"LifeStyle International Christian University"* is the answer to those questions.

He's looking for History Makers.

In His Presence

Apostle Doctor Alan Pateman
(Overseer)

❖

Preface

Our heart and passion behind **"Connecting for Excellence International Apostolic Network"** is to reach out to the world with the gospel, making disciples. It is our passion to raise up the leaders of tomorrow, who will have influence in all realms of authority, men and women of strategy, wisdom, and true godliness, who'll stand with stature and maturity in this hour.

A vision to develop networks of relationships *(apostolic companies)*, which the Holy Spirit is developing, these relationships look for apostolic support and encouragement. In so doing our desire is to encourage the body of Christ to move boldly and powerfully in the supernatural, released to fulfil their divine destinies for the glory of God.

Too many talented and sincere people experience misalignments in their lives, which only serve to quash, distract and take away from God's purpose. Misalignments can only ever take away. However divine connections are a lifeline.

Genuine relationships are not easily come by. They are forged out of life through commitment, time and energy. There is a price to such relationships, but the price is greater still if we don't take the time to ever pursue such connections.

Relationship – can be such a loose word but in the context of ministry or even business you cannot survive without the right connections or contacts. With God involved these become divine connections.

The vision provides the opportunity for:

- Apostolic relationships
- Networking
- Mentoring for ministry development
- Prophetic impartation and integration
- Teaching through LICU
- Making disciples and teaching them to walk in the power of the resurrection
- Ministry Ordination

❖

Introduction

The characteristics of the apostolic will be at the forefront of what God is doing within and through the church at this time. To reveal the heart of God in stirring up and drawing forth the dynamic potential that has been deposited in each born-again believer.

In so doing, exposing the darkness that has for so long gripped the church to become silent, inactive and powerless, therefore our cities, nations and the world remain gripped in the hands of Satan.

At first the apostolic will be strongly resisted but the Spirit of God will bring conviction, the presence of God will be felt everywhere, the atmosphere will be divinely changed as the word of God is preached. Only God's Spirit can reveal the true condition of our hearts.

It is important for all of us to have that (for some rare) intimate communion with God where we can say, like Evan Roberts of the Welsh revival of 1904, "Bend me! Bend me! Bend us!" Evan prayed so fervently that perspiration poured down his face and tears streamed quickly saying, "I am coming, coming Lord to Thee!"

The apostolic is not a popular style, but one that mirrors the lives of many who have dared to live the life of Christ in their day. Those who have taken the inspiration and motivation solely from the fundamental simplicity of the word of God and backed by the power and might of the Holy Spirit.

God is challenging everything that can be challenged. This is the time for the restoration of the apostolic *(Ephesians 4:11)*, the prophetic, the time for the church to rise up and take possession of the land.

The apostolic is in full swing, the best is yet to come, now is the time to take the cities. To take the land with a shout! This has to be the most exciting and privileged time to live in. To be able to see with the eyes of the Spirit, both all that has past and that which is to come. The church, the bride of Christ, will leave this planet in triumph, not in defeat.

❖

CHAPTER 1

Interest and Concerns

It's important to remember that this is part four of *a four book series* of "The Age of the Apostolic Apostleship." The first covers "Laying Foundations," the second "Apostles and the Local Church," the third the "Preparations for Ministry" and the fourth "Developments and Provision," which you are about to read. To understand the context you need to have read books one, two and three.

Our heart and passion behind **"Connecting for Excellence International Apostolic Network"** is for *"A Network of Relationships,"* apostolic companies that the Holy Spirit has and is developing for this **end time move** of God. These relationships look for apostolic support and encouragement. In so doing, our desire is to encourage the men and women of God to move boldly and powerfully in the Holy Spirit. *Being released to fulfil their destinies* for the glory of God.

The Developments and Provision of a Network

This is the linking of people with a common interest or area of concern. As we move on in this New Millennium and apostolic age we will see a new emphasis and the development of denominational and associational networking working together.

Dr. Bill Hamon says, "Networking does not imply that all groups should come under some Pope type figure or apostolic movement. Networking simply implies associations or people with a net such as a fishing net.

Each member of the network is like that of a knot that ties the net together. Those who have vision, grace and wisdom, to network with other networks will become the great fishing net that God will use to draw in the great multitude of souls. This gives the Holy Spirit the opportunity to bring a greater unity and corporate vision within the body of Christ.

This will enable all available resources to be harnessed to work together towards assisting the body of Christ to initiate and sustain an effective thrust towards souls. The common meeting ground is to have the corporate vision of reaping the great end time harvest and proclaiming Jesus Christ as Lord over all the earth" (Hamon 14).

Effectively, the network depends upon people *(pastors and ministers)* who are totally committed in every aspect of their life to the Lord Jesus Christ, people who are willing to use their God given talents and abilities without regard to the cost, with great joy.

Remembering that this relationship of association networking is not to threaten or contradict denominational loyalties or cause division but to help bring strength, depth, unity, clarity, and the word of God that can only enhance better skills and insights into sharing the word of God.

Spiritual Hubs of Government

Their aim is to help establish ministry centres of excellence and significance for this present move of God, Spiritual Hubs of Government that **enhance His kingdom** and to provide a platform for ministry gifts to speak into the cities and nations in an effective way.

To develop ministries, enhancing and bringing them into positions of leadership, to influence every area of society. To combine their skills, experience and abilities, to make increasing individual and corporate impact in the regions of their influence for the *kingdom of God* and for the glory of the Lord Jesus Christ.

The awareness of a situation, need or opportunity will need collaboration of many Christians *(the body of Christ)* from across the different denominational lines in related expertise and location that is required to meet the need. Setting initial meetings with individuals known to identify with the need and clarify the need to pray, share and hear what God is saying.

Of this "Core-Group" making its works known to others, local organisations interested in that activity, and visit others working that field. Introduce the "Core Group," to the media, to assist finding wider support and publicise its work. Offering to make a continued contribution and support in every possible way and linking the "Core Group" to businessmen who can help provide funds, services and expertise. Seek to support and help from the rest of the body.

Network Objectives

To find and bring together apostolic leadership *(Connecting for Excellence)* with a heart for God and a call on their lives, who have a common vision, to enable them to work together with initiatives to promote the kingdom of God in their sphere of work or ministry, providing spiritual support, teaching and training, fellowship and encouragement, advisory and other services relevant. Being a vehicle for the setting up and establishing new works, fellowships, bible schools, and businesses in areas of their location.

This vision in every factor of society taking full advantage of opportunities that is open to Christians in position of leadership and influence, to implement and fulfil their visions. *To advance the Christian faith by the proclamation and furtherance of the gospel of God* concerning His Son Jesus Christ our Lord and the preaching and teaching of the word of God in one's region, town, city, nation and the world.

With the doctrines and articles of belief conducting with the consent *(where possible)* of the relevant authorities, to conduct open-air crusades, to establish apostolic bible schools for ministry development, setting forth a prescribed curriculum and course of study.

To course to be written and printed, or otherwise reproduced and circulated gratuitously or otherwise periodicals, magazines, books, leaflets or other documents or films recorded tapes or by any other media which is or may be available. Raising finance to permit the ongoing of all the above.

Functional Practice

The leaders or overseer of "Connecting for Excellence International Apostolic Network" do not have the right to interfere in the internal running of its individual members or churches, *(elders and pastors are responsible for the local church)* but has the machinery to act and deal with issues and problems on the invitation of members. The senior overseer and boards of directors *DO NOT* hold authoritative power over members or churches.

But within the power of the association or network, speak, act and work for and on behalf of its partners, churches, and ministries of the Christian faith by virtue of the power vested in the association itself. *Remember that which you will find in this book is only a guideline for foundational purposes only.*

Every ministry in the local body of the church has the right, if it so desires to appoint internally for its own intern pastoral convenience. To appoint pastors and officers as they see fit, and such officers or elders are expected to fulfil the duties of that office to which he or she has been appointed internally in his or her own congregation.

This however does not mean that such a person has reached the standard of spiritual development required to be selected for ordination, this is where apostolic oversight comes in. Remember ministers should have at least a Bachelor's degree.

Those who are selected or ordained to any position will have ecumenical, national and international recognition by the "Connecting for Excellence International Apostolic Network."

CHAPTER 2

Apostolic Association Network

As an apostolic network we continue to advise that all fellowships, ministries, church organisations, bible schools etc.; to be in a relationship with an apostolic-association or network. Apostolically no individual part of the body functions without the *flow of life* that comes through being directly joint in unity to the whole body of Christ. Isolation brings a stagnancy and eventual deception.

You have to, however be able to accept the basis and commitment of such an organisational structure. The apostolic presbytery of a said network *(one of)* will provide them with authenticity, a platform of recognition for the force of support, the welfare of its people, evangelisation and the spreading of the gospel. We also as a network urge that *(all)* partners fight *(speak out)* against: Anti-Semitism, racism, sexism, classism, abortion, etc.

Specific Responsibilities

To safeguard and maintain the purity of the nature of the association, is related to the understanding of the *"The Apostolic and Prophetic Movement."*

Boldness, strength, fervency, commitment, strong worship, warfare and intercession, above all living a life of righteousness, holiness, compassion and love *(1 Corinthians 13:1-13)*.

To this end he or she must ensure that wherever they have charge, **that they** impart to the people **and encourage people** to be of the same spirit and mind. Also it must be held that any ministerial or other relationships that may develop, do not conflict or offer hindrances to the unity of the association and its out-working, in either the lives of the main body of the churches or its apostolic relationships.

- To safeguard against division at all times, *"Make every effort to keep the unity of the Spirit through the bond of peace"* *(Ephesians 4:3)*.

- Teaching and exemplifying a life of consecration and holiness. Standing against all unrighteousness *(Leviticus 20:7; Hebrews 12:14; 1 Peter 3:18)*.

- Teach the principles of tithing and the giving of offerings *(seed)* and the giving of alms as essential to pleasing God and receiving the associated blessings, individually and corporately *(Malachi 3:10; Proverbs 28:27; 2 Corinthians 9:6; Galatians 6:7; Matthew 13:8)*.

- Develop relationships with other gifts, pastors etc., enhancing trust, reliability and confidence. Your title is not a job description but a mandate to service.

- Develop true disciples but not at the expense of those who may *not* be ready to respond to the cost of such commitment. Holding fast to the *"no compromise stance,"* yet realising babies don't grow into adults over night.

- Impart the vision for the local community, i.e. evangelism and care etc.

- Help to mobilise the local body *to action* consistent with the vision of God.

- To build whenever possible, relationships with other local leaders, outside of your ministry and association, without loss of the vision and its standards of excellence, not relinquishing spiritual values gained.

- Personal standards and presentation and hygiene must be exemplary. Equally high standards of cleanliness and excellence must be reflected in the homes and all other aspects of the minister's life, i.e. the office, the car etc., *being a standard to others.*

Christian Representation

Note: No church leader or ministry who *invents buys or sells documents* that falsely create the belief that someone is trained or ordained, will not be recognised by this Network Association.

His or her ministry would be seen as undesirable to the Christian faith. Ordained ministers must seek to bring such people to the integrity of the Christian representation.

Restoration is also important, therefore if it is brought to our attention that a pastor or leader is in sin or dealing with feelings of failure or sexual misconduct, marriage difficulties or any other misgivings, and perhaps about to say, "I quit." Then we want to help them.

> *Brethren, if a man is overtaken in any trespass, you who are spiritual restore such a one in a spirit of gentleness, considering yourself lest you also be tempted.*
>
> *(Galatians 6:1 NKJV)*

Sending Progress Report

If any member of the network goes for a period of *"one year"* without sending a progress report, we will see this as *a lack of response or commitment* on their part. We then will send a letter of concern. If this then is ignored we will take it that their desire to be associated with the association has come to a close.

Remember:

"Connecting for Excellence International Apostolic Network of Churches and Ministries in Association" is an "umbrella title" for those in:

- **Association:** i.e. body of persons organised for joint purpose; connection of ideas and fellowship

- **Affiliation:** i.e. "affiliating or being affiliated - order, compelling... help and support." An obligatory relationship between "Connecting for Excellence International Apostolic Network" and "LifeStyle International Christian University," and those affiliated

We have an obligation to help aid and support if one comes under the umbrella of affiliation.

❖

CHAPTER 3

Preventing
Ministry Burnout

According to some studies 1,500 pastors per month quit the ministry. You don't have to be the next statistic. **Therefore the question is,** "Are you guarding your ministry from ministry burnout?"

Ministry Today magazine, which serves and empowers church leaders or Spirit-led ministers, by providing practical, relevant tools for growth, asked Larry Huch what he believes pastors can do to prevent burnout. Here's what he had to say:

Keep Your Priorities Straight

- *First* – God; if I don't have a relationship *with* Him, I can't minister *for* Him

- *Second* is my wife; if I lose her, I lose my destiny
- *Third* are my children; why do we work so hard to get other people into heaven and then ignore our own children?
- *Fourth* is our staff
- *Fifth* is our church

Jesus says that His yoke is easy, and His burden is light. This doesn't mean you don't work hard – you just don't work *"worried."* You have to believe you are going to win and keep the victory. One of the ways you do that is through the right fellowship with others.

Don't sacrifice everything for the church. God does not need that. I know of one man who wants nothing to do with Christianity because even though his father was a pastor and everyone thought he was a great man of God, *he had a mistress.* If the mistress needed carpet, furniture or money, it was there, but if the man's wife or family had a need, it wasn't there. *The "mistress" wasn't a woman – it was the church.*

Don't Let Everyone Dump on You

You cannot let people call you 24 hours a day. My job is to motivate and teach. I have trained my staff to handle various areas of responsibility; they don't come to me with everything. *You have to guard the anointing.*

Know when it's time to step up to a new level. When you're pioneering a church, you do everything. But as the church grows, you have to train people to do the work of the ministry. As a pastor, you need to stay fresh in your relationship with God so you can bring a fresh word to the people.

Don't put people in a position to win their loyalty. Pastors spend too much time trying to lure people in, or back into the church, when these people aren't going to make it anyway – they just want to manipulate you.

Quit baby-sitting Christians and win souls, and you'll stay fresh. If somebody backslides, I'll go after him or her. But not if somebody leaves because they're mad nobody called them. I'm not here to baby-sit. If you're three weeks old, we'll change your diaper; but if you're 30 years old, we have a problem.

Know your calling. Many people who are pastoring churches are doing something they are not called to do. Maybe they're called to be pastors, but not *senior* pastors. If you are not in the right position on the team, it will wear you out.

Take Joe Montana, one of the greatest quarterbacks of all time. If you give him the same ball, the same place, the same game and the same team, but change his number to a line-backer, not only will he not be the best, *he'll die.* He won't make it because he's in the wrong position. You have to know your calling. And no matter how good you are, you have to build the right team around you.

There must be a Mentoring Process for Ministry

Get good training and mentorship. In addition to biblical knowledge, you also need to have other skills, such as people skills and hands-on ministry experience. I like the pattern of some of the large churches in South America.

- *First,* you have to be saved
- *Then* filled with the Spirit
- *Then* able to win people on the streets
- *Then* able to build a cell group, and out of that birth other cell groups
- *Then* you start a church that becomes self-supporting
- *Then* you are brought home, and leadership lays hands on you
- **And then you are called a pastor**

Finally, embrace God's love. God is a good God. He is more interested in you, the worker, than He is in your work. You are not alone. God will build relationships – we are in this together. You will see visions and dreams that were stolen given back.

This is the greatest era the church has ever seen.

❖

CHAPTER 4

Team Ministry

Forbes Magazine once said, "Success is 10% ability, 30% credibility and 60% visibility. Ability + credibility = visibility." Help a person develop their ability to meet the needs of others. When people begin to experience healing through another person, this makes that person's ministry credible.

They will then begin to encourage others to get involved in your ministry. Visibility will be a natural by-product and your ministry will be released to the nations.

Recommend a list of helpful books that will benefit your spiritual sons and daughters develop and take on your spirit. Explain why each is important and have all the team reading the same book for a month. So that everyone is being impacted at the same time, then you can have collective and constructive dialogue.

In addition ensure personal contact each month with every individual on the team. This can be achieved over meals, coffee, prayer times, counselling and recreation time or calls. Possibly, your team is too large for this, so then it's necessary to raise up team leaders or a team pastor who possesses your heart to keep the personal touch in the ministry. Training and development – personal time – maturity!

Recognise spiritual sons and Daughters

- Start praying for and recognise spiritual sons and daughters that God wants to add to your ministry (Matthew 4:18-22; 2 Peter 1:3-11)

- Cultivate parameters and credentials for ministry team participation

- Define and list various areas of duty and potential team involvement

- Pray 1 Chronicles 28:21, "…every willing man of any skill will be with you in all the work for all kinds of service" (NASB)

- Increase the training process of your spiritual sons and daughters, concentrating more upon *impartation* than information (John 5:19,20; John 17:4-8)

Single-mindedness is required for impact. All you do is an employment of time, initiative and resources. The most effective use of your time is to centre it up on the right people who can replicate your heart and ministry. The more people involved in meeting the needs of others, the more others will contribute the resources to meet your operating costs.

The ultimate confirmation of true spiritual fathers is the commissioning of spiritual sons to the nations.

- Jesus did the work and others spectated
- Jesus did the work and others aided
- Others did the work and Jesus spectated!
- Others did the work and Jesus departed

Cultivate clear parameters, strategies, boundaries, and targets for your ministry team (Romans 13; Ephesians 4:22-32). People need to know what is expected and where they stand. 80% of the development of future leaders involves giving them reachable goals, occasion for responsibility, problems to solve and the resources to succeed.

Give each team member a variety of opportunities to serve and prove their ability to handle responsibility. Find out which areas draw the best from them and which draw out the worst. What nurtures their gifts and what kills them.

Growth in the team requires the development of team leaders or pastors (Numbers 11:16, 17). Team leaders are influencers, who people naturally like to follow. They recognise what needs doing and get it done. They are fixers, discerning the needs of each member and are always looking to meet them. They are problem solvers.

Catching the Vision

Team leaders are good managers, who take pleasure in catching the vision of the leader and then motivating others.

Others usually follow them because of the influence of the spiritual father. In other words they are better at managing than leading! Functioning best as a number two rather than a number one. In the kind of support role, that listens to the vision of the spiritual father and then helps to execute it to the max.

The team leader influences the spiritual atmosphere of the whole team. He or she is the one with whom people will most likely be vulnerable and discuss their problems with. They are responsible to ensure that each individual team member walks in the central values of the ministry. Bringing correction where it's needed, with humility and encouragement.

Teachers are gifted with the ability to communicate the deeper things of God in a simple and coherent manner, so that each person is able to comprehend. They are not just distributors of digital information, but midwives that help birth revelation through the act of impartation into the lives of others.

Bringing forth a Ministry

In Luke 1:26-38 we can read the account where the angel Gabriel gave Mary a personal prophecy about bringing forth a ministry (Christ) that would bless the world. The natural process that she had to undergo parallels the spiritual process that we must undergo to bring forth a spiritual baby (ordained ministry).

- Isaiah 66:8 – Zion in labour – then she gives birth
- Romans 8:26 – the Spirit helps us

Prior to the birthing process, we must develop an intimate relationship with God who causes His Spirit to plant seeds of faith and vision, which develop and grow like a baby in the womb of our spirit. Patience and flexibility are required for the long process from conception to delivery.

- James 1:15 – sin is also birthed, when full-grown gives birth to death
- James 1:21 – humbly accept the word planted in you, which can save you

Like an expectant Mary whose womb was stretched, we are stretched until we feel we cannot grow anymore. We become awkward and like the pregnant woman after nine months, we feel that we can take no more! Yet things must get worse before they get better, with the hardest labour pains coming at delivery.

The Twelfth Hour Experience

The 12th hour experience can be drawn out and just before our promise comes forth into the light, we experience our darkest hour of labour and intensity. We are visited with doubting thoughts like, "Why did I ask for this, I don't want to go through with it. It's not worth it!"

Instead, as we flow with the labour pains, before we realize it, the fruit of our labour is revealed! Our ministry comes forth for all to see. And like any new baby, a ministry will go through its first vulnerable years of dependency. As we pour out our lives into it, it will eventually self-advocate. All it will require from us is our parental vision, care, counsel and covering.

Any "success" born outside of due process, will not be able to sustain itself or reach fullest potential (Isaiah 66:7-8).

1) Life		a) Parental vision
2) Energy	in time	b) Care
3) Time		c) Counsel
4) Ability		d) Covering

Discouragement diminishes once you realise - God is moving indeed!

❖

CHAPTER 5

Thoughtful Questions

What is required of me to be a part of the "Connecting for Excellence International Apostolic Network of Churches and Ministries in Association?"

A. You must have some type of relational connection with the Board of Directors whether they are Senior Pastors/Apostles and/or the Senior Overseer.

Q. What type of authoritative jurisdiction am I giving to the "Connecting for Excellence International Apostolic Network" in order for me to become a partner?

A. None as such, it is our belief that each pastor or leader is responsible before God for his or her group of people that has been given to them by God. I.e. it is your ordained ministry. Itinerant ministries on the other hand should be submitting to an apostolic pastor, elders or an apostolic team.

We believe entirely on kingdom structure, whereas one has to ask the question, "Are they a local pastor or some other ministry gift?" (Ephesians 4:11-16)

The ministry gifts are mentioned throughout the bible, but the church as a whole seems to be in total confusion about who's who and where they fit in! And yet no area of ministry has been so well documented, so well developed in the New Testament as the ministry of the apostle.

Scripture is Clear

These apostolic ministries have so often been misunderstood, in fact many people refuse to acknowledge such gifts because of misunderstanding. Just because we neglect or choose to ignore that there is a structure of authority, does not mean that it doesn't exist. This causes great damage in the body of Christ, because the scriptures are clear, that it's these apostolic gifts that prepare God's people for works of service.

If the ministry of an apostle does not function properly within and over, then nothing else will. It has to be said that there is a lot of ambition and rebellion amongst those who have so-called ministries.

They have been raised to go their own way and do what they please with an attitude that says, "No one is going to tell me what to do, this is my ministry and I'm submitting it to no man. I'm serving Jesus!"

You cannot serve Jesus in ministry without submitting to His delegated authority. Remember, if you have the above attitude, you will have problems that you don't need to bear.

When the Holy Spirit speaks to the church and reveals things to the body of Christ, He always brings order and discipline to accomplish His work. Everyone loves a good meeting and enjoys revelation and anointing and power, but dislikes order, reproof, discipline. We need to come to that place where we can enjoy every aspect of God's word.

The apostle and prophet's ministry is of course the foundational gifting that we need to build on and to a great extent deal with the disciplining of the saints. The apostle can see how things should be maintained and developed and to bring order where there is confusion. But many are trying to build their house without foundations that will support all that God desires.

Not Imposing but Order

The apostolic brings order and stability; many might think that the apostolic ministry is imposing. For God's work to be truly established it will require God's strength and order. This is why the ministry of the apostle is as essential as are all the other ministry gifts.

The last portion of Ephesians 4:8 says, "He...gave gifts to men." "He" refers to Jesus, who is the one who gives the gifts and places them in the church (1 Corinthians 12:18).

Despite their different functions, the gifts should work together. Ulf Ekman in his book, "The Apostolic Ministry" says on page 10, "That first we need to realise that the ministry gifts are individuals with a task from heaven, they are gifts to the body of Christ and should be accepted as such. Some consider ministry gifts as a threat, while others become confused and uncertain. But if we want to benefit from them, then we must accept them as they are.

We read in the forth chapter of Ephesians that God wants us to come to a point of spiritual maturity. He wants us to attain to the whole measure of the fullness of Christ, no longer driven by every wind of teaching. The Holy Spirit has the same desire you have for people to be saved and edified, and for God's glory and for the works of Jesus to be made manifest.

God's Ordained Order

He longs to affect the world in a way that makes the kingdom of God 'visible.' This is achieved as the body of Christ is built up through the ministry gifts. However, this is often overlooked and becomes one of the major causes for the problems and attacks against the body of Christ among the ministry gifts.

The enemy strikes here more than anywhere else, because if the ministry gifts don't function, as they should, then neither will anything else. They are an inherent part of God's planed and ordained order.

Some people teach that the ministry gifts are unimportant or unnecessary, as long as everything is functioning well. Everyone needs to be involved in the body of Christ, but this can only happen when the ministry gifts function effectively.

'But this has nothing to do with me! I'm just an ordinary Christian. I'm not called to the ministry gifts.' You're wrong! You still need to recognise God's servants, and discern between true and false in this vital area. You are directly affected whether you have a special calling or not. You need to know and accept how God works through His servants" (Ekman 10-11).

❖

CHAPTER 6

Financial Economy

What is my financial obligation to the "Connecting for Excellence International Apostolic Network?"

A. We teach from Malachi 3:8-10, which tells us to bring our tithes and offerings into the storehouse. You as a pastor or an itinerant ministry would not exist without this financial, biblical, God given teaching. We also teach that the members of our churches should tithe to the church (storehouse) to which the member belongs. Encouraging them from the biblical concept that ten per cent of their income should be their tithe.

It is our belief that if partners of "Connecting for Excellence International Apostolic Network, Churches and Ministries in Association" are serious about their covenant relationship, they would not hesitate to give tithes and offerings to the said mentioned association.

This is a gift set aside monthly to help the association help others. Remember for our partners we are the storehouse.

God's ways of Order of Finance

As mentioned in my book "Preparations for Ministry," chapter nine, "Honouring Your Apostle" that one of the questions that I had for many years regarding finance was in relation to, "Does a leader need to tithe the tithe?" The answer to this is found in Numbers 18:26-29; remember the Levite priests were commanded to pay a tithe from the tithe that they received from the people.

> Speak to the Levites and say to them: "When you receive from the Israelites the tithe I give you as your inheritance, you must present a tenth of that tithe as the Lord's offering. Your offering will be reckoned to you as grain from the threshing-floor or juice from the winepress. In this way you also will present an offering to the LORD from all the tithes you receive from the Israelites. From these tithes you must give the LORD's portion to Aaron (**your apostle**) the priest. You must present as the LORD's portion the best and holiest part of everything given to you."

As in the reference we see in the Old Testament where the priests lived off of the tithe, we then must be clear in our teaching when we teach on the subject of *God's ways of order of finance.* In regard to church leadership or directors of a Christian organization, regardless of terminology, denominational preference or apostolic network the principle being that we teach one thing and then excuse ourselves because of our preference of position – this is completely hypocritical.

Many churches, pastors give offerings – such as to the itinerant ministry that has been ministering in their church. Or to their structural development or outreach project. Of course these things are wonderful but usually these gifts are given in regard to ones own vision.

This is no different for many in relationship to develop one's own business. This is not wrong in itself, God wants us to develop the vision that He has given to us, one encourages members to give to such things *(this will enhance those members)*. Encourage them to tithe and give offerings into the storehouse so that there will be meat in God's house and an open heaven, then the people thereof can prosper. But when one stands back – this in theory looks wonderful, yet actually is also falling into the trap of deception.

In these endtimes not only will there be a greater development of networking, where ministries are concerned, but also the network of the apostolic ministry. I believe that it's important to remain connected, committed and under the right structural covering. For example every leader or pastor needs to be in relationship and accountable.

Not only are individual members called to be responsible in being connected to the body of Christ, i.e. the local church but also each church, leadership, or pastor needs to be connected to the wider body. The flow of God's anointing and blessing comes through connection, apostolic relationship and unity *(Psalms 133:1, 3)*.

What am I saying then?

It's important to teach on tithing but you as an organization or church should also be tithing to whom God has connected you to. You might say, well I'm in relationship to many. Yes, that may be true and certainly correct, **but who is *your* pastor or apostle? Who is the person that you submit yourself to?** This is where you should tithe, the best and holiest part of everything given to you…v29. And I don't mean your wage I mean 10% of the income of the WHOLE of your ministry or church.

This will not only release an open heaven over your ministry, which will flow down through every branch of your vision *(remembering that your tithe opens up the floodgate)*. And then of course your offering that goes to those itinerant ministries etc. will bring a harvest of supply to you and your ministry, which will affect also your people.

You then will be living what you teach. Let me just mention this, more as a statement; there are many that are in ministry that are not pastors or leaders. They might be an evangelist, prophet etc., but what I find as I travel is that pastors have an attitude that their ministry should be the only ministry in the church to receive a wage. They might pay their secretary or heads of departments etc., but what about the apostolic itinerary ministries?

Because what we have is ministry gifts starting churches because they perceive that the only way to finance their ministry is to pastor. What they really needed was to be part of an apostolic team, where the leader considered it his role to make sure that he enhances a balanced ministry. They then can at least have a financial foundation i.e. weekly support – so they can focus on what God has called them to do rather than look to try and survive in the wrong position.

Praise the Lord for true accountability, for honesty, for love, for protection, for wisdom. It all comes from God and we are not to be wading out there all alone without them.

God has made every provision for us to be successful and stay that way and *"not go down in defeat for one split second"* if only we will heed to His voice and obey His wisdom found in His word. All we need is there – that's where our motto originates from – *"His voice is all the provision you need."* Because every guideline – plumb line – guiding fork and instruction manual is right there in the word of God. If we fall short, we fall short of our knowledge of that word or our willingness to obey it!

Q. What if I am already financially supporting other organisations?

A. "Connecting for Excellence International Apostolic Network" is not looking to be the only organisation that you are involved with. As you will discover from part one, two and three of these books, "The Age of Apostolic Apostleship." You can be a partner that is in association, i.e. being part of a body of persons organised for joint purpose, connection or ideas and fellowship.

Q. Where do my monthly contributions *(seed)* to the association network go?

A. Your monthly support is separated into several categories; firstly there is of course the administration of any organisation. The expense of stationery and printing of what you find in your hands. Also travelling expenses for the senior overseer, to those churches and ministries who are diligently looking to be faithful, this has to be shown through their consistency of pushing into the said organisation.

Endtime devastations, flooding, earthquakes, fire etc., or the economy that has escalated or collapsed. We find this problem of collapsed economy in many countries around the would, I know in Uganda for instance, where we help a number of churches, that the tithes and offerings from these village churches hardly produce any currency at all, just enough to feed perhaps a pastor.

In these cases I might add we must do our utmost to help as God directs (Romans 15:23-28).

CHAPTER 7

Ministry Ordination

Can the "Connecting for Excellence International Apostolic Network" ordain me?

A. Yes. There is a two-level plan *(in theory)*, of and leading up to ordination. Firstly, you have to become a "partner" of "Connecting for Excellence International Apostolic Network," *(there needs to be a relationship first)* and then you can apply for ordination.

Increasing numbers of men and women in full time ministry have been ordained, receiving ordination. I have had the pleasure of ordaining some five hundred people to date of this book as a result of the apostolic ministry – and we are now seeing their ministries and churches multiply, growing in strength and maturity.

For example Pastor Luke of the "Royal Priesthood Mission Centre International," Kenya, wrote and said, "your teachings and general interaction in ministry was fatherly, what we saw was the true mark of an apostle. As a matter of fact we have been praying to God to give us a man with an apostolic calling to oversee our church and many that the Lord will lead us to pioneer. We being an independent ministry need someone we can look to for advise and can speak insight into our lives as the Lord directs him."

The church in Kenya can also enable a National Platform, where other apostolic ministries can gather and be heard. This will enhance leadership. My heart is not to take from but to serve these leaders, providing platforms, with teaching seminars etc., celebration meetings and the development of a world class Christian University, LifeStyle International with extension campuses.

Q. Do I have to do away with or disconnect from my affiliation with other organisations that I am already ordained with in order to join "Connecting for Excellence International Apostolic Network?"

A. No. This is not a denomination although it is a structure, nor is it a dictatorship. What we desire is an affiliation of association in relationship to what the Spirit of God is doing and saying. Our purpose is not to gain control. Apostolic ministries are not meant to have a Pope-like figure at the point of some triangle. This ministry is foundational and will enhance your foundations. It's to focus your attention to ministry growth and development, helping you to become established as a ministry of excellence, to obtain all that God has for you.

When one is ordained the following items shall be provided *(if requested)*,

- Letter of recognition
- Certificate
- Ministers identification card; this is to help with hospital visitation i.e.
- Apostle Doctor Alan Pateman's four books on The Age of Apostleship, on behalf of "Connecting for Excellence International Apostolic Network, Churches and Ministries in Association."

❖

CHAPTER 8

What is Ordination?

Ordination is a biblical principle and directive that is found throughout both the Old and New Testaments. It can be seen in operation first of all in the Garden of Eden and then repeatedly during every spiritual awakening right through to the Acts of the Apostles and the early church. There is however, reference to ordination before this time by the prophet Ezekiel, where he says of Lucifer,

> *You were anointed as a guardian cherub, for so I ordained you. You were on the holy mount of God; you walked among the fiery stones.*
>
> *(Ezekiel 28:14)*

He prophesies concerning Satan that, prior to his rebellion and fall, he was ordained *(or set in place)* by God as an anointed cherub on the holy mount of God.

This pre-time prophetic revelation serves to show the importance of ordination within the kingdom and body of the Lord Jesus Christ. His rejection due to pride, led to rebellion, violence and disorder.

...God is not a God of disorder...
(1 Corinthians 14:33)

The importance and reason for **ordaining ministers is fundamental** to the nature and character of God. He loves order - He created it and used it to bring to birth the world and everything in it - including mankind. He ordained light and darkness. He ordained earth and sky, land and sea and in so doing provided a structured environment for mankind.

Now the Lord God had planted a garden in the East, in Eden; and there he put the man he had formed.
(Genesis 2:8)

When God put Adam in the Garden of Eden, the **wording used implies appointment or ordination.** Adam was firstly appointed to a position provided and prepared for him; later on in verse 15, God completes the call by defining his responsibility i.e. to *"work it"* *(the garden)* and take care of it.

The principle itself is that of one who has authority, *delegating to another a commission of responsibility and therefore a realm of spiritual authority.* It is the highest form of *"service"* within the body of Christ. Jesus said, *"He who would be chief among you, would be the servant of all!"*

There are different degrees of ordination as there are different measures of service. Ordination therefore can be defined thus:

- The appointment of an individual to a place or position of authority

- The delegation to an individual of an area of responsibility; Moses ordained elders to assist in the management of the mighty nation of Israel

He chose capable men from all Israel and made them leaders of the people, officials over thousands, hundreds, fifties and tens.

(Exodus 18:25)

He also ordained the priesthood, with Aaron as high priest.

Have Aaron your brother brought to you from the Israelites, with his sons Nadab and Abihu, Eleazar and Ithamar, so that they may serve me as priests.

(Exodus 28:1)

Towards the end of his life and ministry he ordained Joshua - his disciple - to be his successor.

So the Lord said to Moses, "Take Joshua son of Nun, a man in whom is the spirit, and lay your hand on him. Make him stand before Eleazar the priest and the entire assembly and commission him in their presence. Give him some of your authority so that the whole Israelite community will obey him. He is to stand before Eleazar the priest, who will obtain decisions for him by inquiring of the Urim before the Lord. At his command, he and the entire community of the Israelites will go out, and at his command they will come in..."

Moses did as the Lord commanded him. He took Joshua and made him stand before Eleazar the priest and the whole assembly. Then he laid his hands on him and commissioned him, as the Lord instructed through Moses.
(Numbers 27:18-23)

The pattern continues with Samuel and David, Elijah and Elisha and many others, each exemplifying ordination as God's purpose for their day. Then Jesus speaking to His disciples states quite clearly that He chose and ordained them to go and bear fruit.

*You did not choose me, but I chose you and **appointed** you to go and bear fruit - fruit that will last - then the Father will give you whatever you ask in my name.*
(John 15:16)

When speaking to Peter after His resurrection. He commissions Peter to feed and take care of His sheep. In every instance mentioned, each individual had laid aside their own will and desire to take up and submit to, the will and desire of God. In so doing, they fulfilled their destiny and call, to powerful effect!

Q. If I am ordained as a part of the "Connecting for Excellence International Apostolic Network, Churches and Ministries Association," can I *(my church or ministry)* benefit from the association's non-profit/trust/charitable status?

A. Yes, yet only if you are in one of the nations within which we have an CFE Office. We encourage every member or organisation whether you are a pastor, an itinerant ministry, group, bible school etc., to apply for their-own non-profit or charitable trust status that is legal within one's own country.

❖

CHAPTER 9

Covenant Partnership

C an I be a partner only of the "Connecting for Excellence International Apostolic Network, Churches and Ministries in Association?"

A. Yes. "Partnership is not a new idea nor is it just a new way to raise money. It is a systematic method, or ordinance, initiated by God, to bring a manifestation of increase into every area of the life of every believer" (Roberts Liardon).

Being a covenant partner has its benefits, like special offers on all book and audio material, reserved seating at CFE conferences, our staff and of course Jenny and I praying for you on a regular basis. We want you to be blessed, healthy, and full of the Holy Spirit and of course strong in faith.

To be a covenant partner you will also receive a Quarterly Newsletter *(Hearing His Voice)* that you will find full of news and encouragement. Just remember that every person who is saved, healed, delivered and touched by the power of God through this ministry has you to thank. Why? Because, when you link up with us at CFE in Covenant Partnership you literally become part of the work that we are doing.

Remember covenant partnership is a relationship where we both work toward the same goal for everyone's good. It is a commitment of both parties standing together in faith, joining their resources to accomplish a common goal or vision.

Perfect Opportunity

Perhaps you have wanted to go to the nations and to somehow be part of what God is doing in the world today and not known how! Well, here is your perfect opportunity! By supporting this ministry both financially and prayerfully, it can be just as rewarding for you as if you had been to the nations personally, (Matthew 10:41-42).

You don't miss out on any of the excitement because all of the testimony and all of the experience, stories and knowledge gained on trips will be brought back and given to you through our newsletter! (Romans 8:37)

Living life at home and yet still being active in the rest of the world at the same time! All it takes is money that's all, and with a little help from our friends we'll go all over the world with God's word, God's power, God's healing and God's love.

We are believing for an army of 10,000 PARTNERS who will faithfully pray and support with their finance this ministry and association on a monthly basis *(50 Euros a month)*. Nothing can stop us if we stand together – there is power in agreement!

❖

CHAPTER 10

Responsive Thoughts

Will we receive regular updates and addresses of all member churches and ministries for relationship purposes and the invitation of those in the itinerant apostolic ministry team?

A. There should be on a yearly basis an update (report) of the ministry, changes that have been made, new members etc. This is separate from the newsletter called "Truth for the Journey." But you are welcome to write in for any details on any of the above.

Q. Are there any rules that I need to be aware of?

A. Yes as you have already discovered, but in this section let me suggest a number one rule in everything you do; and that is, *"to hear the Voice of the Lord."*

Q. Can we introduce or recommend fellow colleagues to this network?

A. As it has already been stated we believe that all local pastors / ministry gifts should be involved within some kind of structure. Therefore encourage all those isolated and yet gifted men and women to be involved in what we believe a true Network of Association should entail.

Q. Can we write or ring directly to the senior apostle?

A. Yes, of course it is important to be able to speak to the Senior Overseer, but this needs to be directed through one of the directors, two to three days before, so that no inconvenience is caused. Please state general concern or question. Then you will be instructed to "a given time." This is not to delay or put you off, it is out of respect as Apostle Alan is very busy. Writing (or email) usually is a better way of contact; letters can be sent directly to the international address.

Q. Do I need to be at an annual CFE apostolic, national or international conference?

A. Yes please. It is important for all associate ministers to be part of a national conference. For one, we have at these conferences, teaching for pastors and leaders. This is where impartation can be given, yearly updates, apostolic relationships built. Also it is of the utmost importance to encourage as many of your people to attend, as this builds unity and fervour for the upcoming months.

Q. How does one apply?

A. Your application form is available on our website, www.cfeapostolicnetwork.com, please see instructions in the back of this book. The form needs to be sent to the International Head Offices. We will need three passport photos with your application; one of these is for the minister's identification card, if you desire one.

❖

CHAPTER 11

Theological Education

C an you explain what **"LifeStyle International Christian University"** is all about and do I have to attend?

A. Seasons might be changing but God's word remains the same. My heart is to help train, equip and be a blessing to those men and women who will be willing to fulfil their potential in ministry and be properly equipped for service. We desire for you to walk and live in the authority and power of God's word and His precious Holy Spirit.

Theological education is held for ministers and lay people alike. This is an interdenominational apostolic ministry of the Holy Spirit. Degrees offered at our university range from a "Diploma in Theology" to a "Doctor of Philosophy" for those who decide to go through the full university program. Remember, Christian believers are called by God to mature spiritually and to have an active (LifeStyle) part in Christian service regardless of their status.

It's undeniable that in today's world, recognized education has become indispensable; therefore it is our desire to offer well-balanced and well-structured courses. Those that have been written by gifted and talented ministers of God, who seek to be inspired by God's word and His Holy Spirit.

Excellent Curriculum

Consequently we have put together an **excellent curriculum**, designed both for correspondence students and extension campuses, which is a strategy to reach the distant learner, whether provincial, national or international.

Teaching and equipping people to reach their divine destiny in God is the main focus of "Connecting for Excellence International Apostolic Network." With hundreds of students trained throughout the globe.

So, it's without any fear of contradiction that we say this is a growing platform, where men and women of dignity and passion can grow and be established in their God given endeavours. As God is the healer of the nations, we pray and believe that many of our alumni will go on to **become world changers** in their own right.

And yes you need to consider becoming one of our international students! It would be our privileged to welcome you from around the world to LifeStyle International Christian University.

Your Advantages:

- Internationally recognised credits
- Opportunity to complete your Diploma, Associate, Bachelor, Master and Doctoral degree!
- Affordable student tuition through our one course one payment scheme
- Incentives and free tuition for every one who finds 5 paying students
- Up to 70% scholarships
- Practical tools to release students into their destinies
- Relevant studies
- Helping to equip students for life and ministry
- Teaching syllabuses authored by internationally well-known teachers
- **HONORARY DEGREES available!**
- And Ordination

❖

CHAPTER 12

The Apostolic
Doctrines, Articles of Belief

Apostle Doctor Christian Harfouche says, "From the first years of the Church — as the Apostles gave themselves to prayer and the ministry of the Word, as the New Testament Scriptures were inspired, confirmed, written, and distributed, the earliest Church communities in Jerusalem, Antioch, and beyond developed certain scriptural statements of faith, creeds.

Some were very simple, others more complex, however for centuries, all over the world, these words of confirmation and agreement were spoken by the Body of Christ, preserving and transmitting the true Orthodoxy — or right way — of the Apostolic Doctrine, the Faith delivered to us.

In the three-hundreds, the Church consolidated and amplified these creeds into a single, universally-accepted statement of the quintessential Christian Faith. The result was a singular Creed, accepted and promulgated by a worldwide gathering of Christian leaders, representing every Christian community spread across the globe.

This ecumenical, pre-denominational unity and agreement continued to transmit and impart a scriptural record of understanding that confirms unequivocally that our Apostolic Faith stands upon the original First Century Faith of the Church of Jerusalem, the Church of Antioch, and the Christian Faith as it is expressed and believed to date by all genuine Christian families worldwide" (globalrevival. com/about/statement-of-faith).

Statement of Faith

The programme of activities of the ministry of CFE shall be based upon and at all times shall be consistent with the following beliefs and statement of faith:

The Scriptures Inspired:

The scriptures, both the Old and the New Testament, are verbally inspired of God and are the revelation of God to man, the infallible, authoritative rule of faith and conduct *(2 Timothy 3:15-17, 1 Thessalonians 2:13, 2 Peter 1:21).*

The One True God:

The one true God has revealed Himself as the eternally self-existent "I AM" the creator of heaven and earth and the redeemer of mankind. He has further revealed Himself as embodying the principles of relationship and association as Father, Son and Holy Ghost *(Deuteronomy 6:4; Isaiah 43:10-11; Matthew 28:29; Luke 3:22)*.

The Deity of the Lord Jesus Christ:

The Lord Jesus Christ is the eternal Son of God. The scriptures declare:

- His virgin birth *(Matthew 1:23; Luke 1:31-35)*
- His sinless life *(Hebrews 7:26; 1 Peter 2:22)*
- His miracles *(Acts 2:22; 10:38)*
- His substitutionary work on the cross *(1 Corinthians 15:3; 2 Corinthians 5:21)*
- His bodily resurrection from the dead *(Matthew 28:6; Luke 24:39; 1 Corinthians 15:4)*
- His exaltation to the right hand of God *(Acts 1:9,11; 2:33; Philippians 2:9-11; Hebrews 1-3)*

The Fall of Man:

Man was created good and upright, for God said, "Let us make man in our image, after our likeness." However, man, by voluntary transgression fell, and thereby incurred not only physical death but also spiritual death, which is separation from God *(Genesis 1:26, 27; 2:17; 3:6; Romans 5:12-19)*.

The Salvation of Man:

Man's only hope of redemption is through the shed blood of Jesus Christ the Son of God.

- Conditions of Salvation:
  Salvation is received through repentance toward
  God and faith toward the Lord Jesus Christ. By the
  washing of regeneration and renewing of the Holy
  Ghost, being justified through faith, man becomes an
  heir of God according to the hope of eternal life *(Luke
  24:47; John 3:3; Romans 10:13-15; Ephesians 2:8; Titus
  2:11; 3:5-7).*

- The Evidence of Salvation:
  The inward evidence of Salvation is the direct witness
  of the Spirit *(Romans 8:16).*

  The outward evidence to all men is a life of righteousness and true holiness *(Ephesians 4:24; Titus 2:12).*

The Ordinances of The Church:

- Baptism in Water:
  The ordinance of baptism by immersion is
  commanded in the scriptures. All who repent and
  believe of the Christ as Saviour and Lord are to be
  baptised. Thus they declare to the world that they
  have died with Christ and that they also have been
  raised with Him to walk in newness of life *(Matthew
  28:19; Mark 16:16; Acts 10:47-48; Romans 6:4).*

- The Holy Communion:
  The Lord's Supper consisting of the elements – bread
  and the fruit of the vine – is the symbol expressing
  our sharing the divine nature of our Lord Jesus Christ
  (2 Peter 1:4), a memorial of His suffering and death
  (1 Corinthians 11:26), and is enjoined on all believers
  "...till He come."

The Baptism in the Holy Spirit:

All believers are entitled to and should ardently expect and earnestly seek the promise of the Father, the baptism in the Holy Ghost and fire, according to the command of our Lord Jesus Christ.

This was the normal experience of all in the early Christian Church. With it comes the endowment of power for life and service, the bestowal of the gifts and their uses in the work of the ministry *(Luke 24:49; Acts 1:4,8; 1 Corinthians 12:1-31).*

This experience is distinct from and subsequent to the experience of the new birth *(Acts 8:12-17; 19:44-46; 11:14-16; 15:7-9).* With the baptism in the Holy Ghost comes such experience as an ever-flowing fullness of the Spirit *(John 7:37-39; Acts 4:8)* and a more active love for Christ, for His word and for the lost *(Mark 16:20).*

The Evidence of the Baptism in the Holy Spirit:

The baptism of believers in the Holy Ghost is witnessed by the initial physical sign of speaking with other tongues as the Spirit of God gives them utterance *(Acts 2:4).* The speaking in tongues in this instance, is the same in essence as the gift of tongues *(1 Corinthians 12:4-10, 28),* but different in purpose and use.

Sanctification:

Sanctification is an act of separation from that which is evil and of dedication unto God *(Romans 12:1; 1 Thessalonians 4:23; Hebrews 13:12).* The scriptures teach a life of "holiness without which no man shall see the Lord" *(Hebrews 12:14),* and by the power of the Holy Spirit we are able to obey the command *"Be ye holy, for I am holy" (1 Peter 1:15, 16).*

Sanctification is realised in the believer by recognising his identification with Christ in His death and resurrection and by faith reckoning daily upon the fact that union and by offering every faculty continually to the dominion of the Holy Spirit *(Romans 6:1-11,13; 8:1,2,13; Galatians 2:20; Philippians 2:12-13; 1 Peter 1:5).*

The Church:

The Church is the body of Christ, the habitation of God through the Spirit with divine appointments for the fulfilment of her great commission. Each believer, born of the Spirit, is an integral part of the General Assembly and Church of the first-born, which are written in heaven *(Ephesians 1:22-23; 2:22; Hebrews 12:23).*

The Ministry:

A divinely called and scripturally ordained ministry has been provided by our Lord for a two-fold purpose:

- The Evangelization of the World
- The edifying of the body of Christ *(Mark 16:15-20; Ephesians 4:11-13)*

Divine Healing:

Divine healing is an integral part of the gospel. Deliverance from sickness is provided for in the atonement and is the privilege of all believers *(Isaiah 53:4-5; Matthew 8:16-17; James 5:14-16).*

The Blessed Hope:

The second coming of Christ includes the rapture of the saints which is one blessed hope, followed by the visible return of Christ with his saints to reign on the earth for one thousand years *(Zechariah 14:5; Matthew 24:27-30; Revelation 1:7; 19:11-14; 20:1-6).*

This millennial reign will bring salvation of national Israel *(Ezekiel 37:21-22; Zephaniah 3:19-20; Romans 11:26-27)* and the establishment of universal peace *(Isaiah 11:6-9; Psalms 72:3-8; Micah 4:3-4).*

The Final Judgement:

There will be a final judgement in which the wicked dead will be raised and judged according to their works. Whosoever is not found written in the Book of Life, together with the devil and his angels, the beast and the false prophet, will be consigned to everlasting punishment in the lake, which burneth with fire and brimstone, which is the second death *(Matthew 9:43-48; Revelation 19:20; 20:11-15; 21:8).*

The Heaven and the New Earth:

We according to his promise, look for new heavens and a new earth, wherein dwelleth righteousness.
(2 Peter 3:13; Revelation 21:22)

Ordinances:

The ordinance of baptism by immersion in water *(Matthew 28:19)* shall be administered to all those who have repented of their sins and who have believed of the Lord Jesus Christ to the saving of their souls, and who give clear evidence of their salvation *(Romans 6:3-5, Colossians 2:12).*

The ordinance of the Lord's Supper shall be observed regularly as enjoined in the scriptures *(Luke 22:19-20; 1 Corinthians 11:23-26).*

❖

Apply Today

Please go to our Connecting for Excellence International Apostolic Network website at www.cfeapostolicnetwork.com, where you can find the **Application Form** as a PDF file on the "Services" page.

When you click on the link, the PDF document <u>downloads automatically</u> unto your computer or device, from where you can <u>print</u> out the form.

Once you have <u>filled</u> all pages, you may return your form along with **three passport photos** to our Head Office *(please see address details enclosed on the form)*. Alternatively you may scan and submit your form as a PDF file to our email address at info@cfeapostolicnetwork.com.

Please also remember to click on the link for the **Minister Recommendation** letters *(which are found on the same page)*. Please give one of these letters to your Pastor or someone credentialed/ordained in full-time ministry, the other two recommendations also need to be completed by ministers; one of which would be accepted by a friend or someone you have known for at least 3 years.

Website: www.cfeapostolicnetwork.com
Email: info@cfeapostolicnetwork.com

❖

Bibliography

- Ekman, Ulf. <u>The Apostolic Ministry</u>. Copyright © 1995. Published by Word of Life Publications. Printed in Sweden.

- Hamon, Bill. <u>Apostles, Prophets and the Coming Moves of God</u>. Copyright © 1997. Published by Destiny Image Publishers, Inc. Printed in USA.

- Unless otherwise indicated, all scriptural quotations are from the HOLY BIBLE, NEW INTERNATIONAL VERSION ®. NIV ®. Copyright © 1973, 1978, 1984 by the International Bible Society. Used by permission of Zondervan Publishing House. All rights reserved.

- Scripture references marked NASB are taken from New American Standard Bible®, Copyright © 1960, 1962, 1963, 1968, 1971, 1972, 1973, 1975, 1977, 1995 by The Lockman Foundation. Used by permission.

- Scripture references marked NKJV are taken from the New King James Version. Copyright © 1982 by Thomas Nelson, 1982 by Thomas Nelson, Inc. Used by permission. All rights reserved.

❖

Resources on the Apostolic Prophetic Ministry

- Abboud, Michael, and Brooke Mackie and Victor Korabelnifkoff. <u>Canaan Land Prophetic Journal #94. "Comest Thou in Peace?"</u> Australia: Canaan Land Publications, 1994.

- Arnott, John. <u>The Father's Blessing</u>. Orlando, Florida: Creation House, 1995.

- Basham, Don. <u>True and False Prophets</u>. Grand Rapids, Michigan: Chosen Books, 1986.

- Cannistraci, David. <u>The Gift of the Apostle</u>. Ventura, California: Regal Books, 1979.

- Chadwick, Henry. <u>The Early Church</u>. England: Penguin Books, 1967.

- Conner, Kevin J. <u>The Church in the New Testament</u>. Australia: Acacia Press, 1982.

- Crist, Terry. <u>A Time of War</u>. Tulsa, Oklahoma: Terry Crist Ministries, 1986.

- Crist, Terry. <u>Interceding Against the Powers of Darkness</u>. Tulsa, Oklahoma: Terry Crist Ministries, 1991.

- Crist, Terry. Warring According to Prophecy. Tulsa, Oklahoma: Whitaker House, 1989.

- Deere, Jack. Surprised by the Voice of God. Grand Rapids, Michigan: Zondervan Publishing, 1996.

- Eckhardt, John. The Apostolic Church. Chicago, Illinois: Crusader Ministries, 1996.

- Eckhardt, John. The Ministry Anointing of the Apostle. Chicago, Illinois: Crusader Publications, 1993.

- Ekman, Ulf. The Apostolic Ministry – Can the Church Live Without It? Word of Life Publishing Sweden. Kingsway Publications LTD UK, 1996.

- Ekman, Ulf. The Church of the Living God. Uppsala, Sweden: Word of Life Publications, 1994.

- Ekman, Ulf. The Prophetic Ministry. Uppsala, Sweden: Word of Life Publications, 1990.

- Gay, Robert. Silencing the Gates of the Enemy. Lake Mary, Florida: Creation House, 1993.

- Hamon, Bill. Prophetic Destiny and the Apostolic Reformation. Santa Rosa Beach, Florida: Christian International Publishing, 1997.

- Hamon, Bill. Prophets and Personal Prophecy. Shippensburg, Pennsylvania: Destiny Image, 1990.

- Hamon, Bill. Prophets, Pitfalls and Principles. Shippensburg, Pennsylvania: Destiny Image, 1991.

- Hamon, Bill. Prophets and the Prophetic Movement. Shippensburg, Pennsylvania: Destiny Image, 1987.

- Hamon, Bill. The Eternal Church. Santa Rosa Beach, Florida: Christian International Publishers, 1981.

- Harfouche, Christian. Authority Over the Powers of Darkness. Shalimar, Florida: Christian Publications, 1993.

- Harfouche, Christian. The Miracle Ministry of the Prophet. Shalimar, Florida: Christian Publications, 1993.

- Harrison, Everet F. The Apostolic Church. Grand Rapids, Michigan: Eerdmans, 1985.

- Hawtin, George R. "The Ministry of the Apostle." The Sharon Star (April/May 1951).

- Jacobs, Cindy. The Voice of God. Ventura, California: Regal Books, 1995.

- LaCoss, Lee. I Will Build My Church. Ørum, Denmark: Lychnos Publishing, 2001.

- Lockyer, Herbert. All the Apostles of the Bible. Grand Rapids, Michigan: Zondervan Publishing, 1972.

- Marocco, James. The Invisible War. Kahulu, Hawaii: Bartemaeus Publishing, 1992.

- McBirnie, William Steuart. The Search for the Twelve Apostels. Wheaton, Illinois: Tyndale House, 1978.

- Mohabir, Philip. Hands of Jesus. Denmark: Powerhouse Publishing, 2003.

- Pickett, Fuchsia. For Such a Time as This. Shippensburg, Pennsylvania: Destiny Image, 1992.

- Pickett, Fuchsia. God's Dream. Shippensburg, Pennsylvania: Destiny Image, 1991.

- Pickett, Fuchsia. Presenting the Holy Spirit. Shippensburg, Pennsylvania: Destiny Image, 1994.

- Pickett, Fuchsia. The Next Move of God. Orlando, Florida: Creation House, 1994.

- Sapp, Roger. The Last Apostles on Earth. Shippensburg, Pennsylvania: Companion Press, 1995.

- Schidler, Bill. The New Testament Church and Its Ministries. Portland, Oregon: Bible Temple, 1980.

- Schultz, Steve. Mentoring & Fathering. Santa Rosa Beach, Florida: Companion Press, 1996.

- Schultz, Steve. Radical Warriors Require Radical Training. Santa Rosa Beach, Florida: D. Steven Schultz, 1991.

- Schultz, Steve. <u>Restoration of the Modern-day Prophet</u>. Santa Rosa Beach, Florida: D. Stephen Schultz, 1990.

- Sheets, Dutch. <u>Intercessory Prayer</u>. Centura, California: Regal Books, 1996.

- Stebins, J.E. <u>Moses and the Prophets; Christ and the Apostles; Fathers & Martyrs</u>. Herlbut, Kellogg & Co., Hartford, Connecticut: American Subscription Publishing House, 1861.

- Thigpen, Travis. <u>Prophetic Evangelism: A Course on Spirit-Led Witnessing</u>. Richmond, Virginia: Travis Thigpen, 1996.

- Wagner, C. Peter. <u>Blazing the Way</u>. Ventura, California: Regal Books, 1995.

- Wagner, C. Peter. <u>Confronting the Powers</u>. Ventura, California: Regal Books, 1979.

- Wagner, C. Peter. <u>Lighting the World</u>. Ventura, California: Regal Books, 1995.

- Wagner, C. Peter. "<u>New Equipment for the Final Thrust</u>," Ministers Today Orlando, Florida: Strang Communications, (January/February 1994).

- Wagner, C. Peter. <u>Spreading the Fire</u>. Ventura, California: Regal Books, 1979.

- Wyatt, Kenneth. <u>The Apostles</u>. Amarillo, Texas: Y-8 Publishing Company, 1989.

❖

Ministry Profile

Doctor Alan Pateman, an apostle, is the President and Founder of **"Alan Pateman Ministries International"** (APMI), which was established in England back in 1987, a Christian-based *(parachurch)* non-profit and non-denominational outreach. This ministry is now focusing in two main areas: First **"Connecting for Excellence"** Apostolic Networking (CFE) and secondly, the teaching arm, **"LifeStyle International Christian University"** (LICU).

CFE is a multi-facetted missions organisation with the purpose of connecting leaders for divine opportunities and building lasting relationships, to touch the lives of leaders literally the world over. Apostle Dr Alan Pateman has to date ordained more than 500 ministers in over 50 NATIONS. In addition there are ministries, churches and schools who are in Association or Affiliation, looking to him for apostolic counsel and oversight.

Secondly LICU, which was founded in 2007, is a study program to help people discover their purpose and destiny. A global network of university campuses and correspondence students, demonstrating the Supernatural Kingdom of God through Doctrinal, Apostolic and Prophetic Teaching. Dr Alan holds the position of President/CEO, Professor of Theology, Biblical Studies and Apostolic Ministry. LICU is exploding throughout Europe, Asia and Africa, enhancing the Body of Christ

Dr Alan has authored more than 35 books including numerous teaching materials and LICU university courses (30) along with hundreds of Truth for the Journey articles on kingdom lifestyle *(that are regularly distributed globally via the internet).*

He is recognised as an Apostle, Bishop, Leadership Mentor, University Educator, Motivational Speaker, Connector and Author, who has also been featured on national and international TV and radio networks throughout the years.

Currently Apostle Alan, his wife Dr Jennifer reside in Lucca *(Tuscany)* Italy and travel out from their Apostolic Company.

- Alan Pateman Ph.D., D.Min., D.D., M.A., B.Th.

Academic Background

Dr. Alan Pateman attended several colleges throughout his training *(including studying Theology at Roffey Place, Horsham, UK and a Member of Kerygma - with Rev. Colin Urquhart and Dr. Bob Gordon - 1985-1987)* before being awarded a Doctorate of Divinity *(2006)* in recognition of his lifetime achievements by the International College of Excellence, now "DanEl Christian College" *(President: Dr. Robb Thompson USA)* also "Life Christian University" *(Dr. Douglas Wingate USA)* where he also earned a Bachelor of Theology B.Th. *(2006),* a Master of Arts in Theology M.A., a Doctor of Ministry in Theology D.Min., *(2007)* and Doctor of Philosophy in Theology Ph.D. *(2013)* from LICU.

❖

To Contact the Author

Please email:

Alan Pateman Ministries International

Email: apostledr@alanpateman.com
Web: www.AlanPatemanMinistries.com

*Please include your prayer requests
and comments when you write.*

❖

Books in this Series

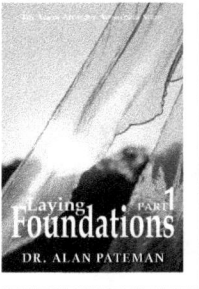

Laying Foundations (Apostleship Series) Part One

In order to view how the Apostolic baton was successfully passed from one generation to the next. Knowing that through the perseverance and obedience of others - history as we know it was altered forever. Therefore it is my desire to encourage all those that are part of Connecting for Excellence to have a solid foundation, insight and teaching that will propel them into God's divine purposes.

ISBN: 978-1-909132-56-6, Pages: 140,
Format: Paperback, Published: 2017
Also available in eBook format!

Apostles and the Local Church (Apostleship Series) Part Two

I want to continue from my first book of this series, four in all, and look at the relationship that should exist between the apostle and the local church - how they should relate and how the authoritative structure within the church works. Also we will look at gifts - for example, is an apostle a position of "office" or "gift"?

ISBN: 978-1-909132-58-0, Pages: 128,
Format: Paperback, Published: 2017
Also available in eBook format!

Preparations for Ministry
(Apostleship Series) Part Three

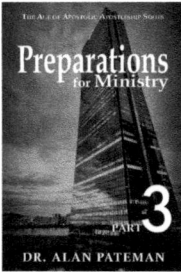

Preparations for Ministry is not something that many want to face. There is an expectation for a trophy for participation, but advice, oversight and years of preparation are necessary to achieve the goals that God has set before us.

ISBN: 978-1-909132-60-3, Pages: 128, Format: Paperback, Published: 2017
Also available in eBook format!

Developments and Provision
(Apostleship Series) Part Four

It's important to remember that this is part four of *a four book series* of "The Age of the Apostolic Apostleship." The first covers "Laying Foundations," the second "Apostles and the Local Church," the third the "Preparations for Ministry" and the fourth "Developments and Provision," which you are about to read. To understand the context you need to have read books one, two and three.

ISBN: 978-1-909132-62-7, Pages: 108, Format: Paperback, Published: 2017
Also available in eBook format!

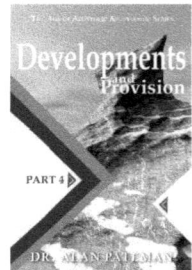

❖

Other Books

Media, Spiritual Gateway

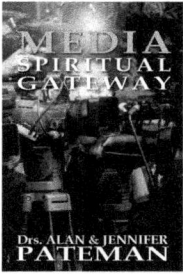

Let's face it; we live in the era of fake news! It's always existed, but never been quite so prominent. Today it's an all-out-war between fact and political fiction.

ISBN: 978-1-909132-54-2, Pages: 192, Format: Paperback, Published: 2018
Also available in eBook format!

Millennial Myopia, From a Biblical Perspective

The standard for every generation is Jesus. However Millennial Myopia describes the trap of focusing everything on one particular generation or demographic cohort, at the exclusion and expense of all others. The Church cannot afford to make this mistake too.

ISBN: 978-1-909132-67-2, Pages: 216, Format: Paperback, Published: 2017
Also available in eBook format!

Truth for the Journey Books

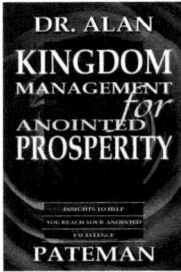

Kingdom Management for Anointed Prosperity

In his book, "Kingdom Management for Anointed Prosperity," Dr. Alan Pateman reveals how we can avoid living in continual crisis due to mismanagement. Life happens to all of us, but how we handle it matters most. "Well done, good and faithful servant! You have been faithful with a few things; I will put you in charge [as manager] of many things. Come and share your master's happiness!" (Matthew 25:21)

ISBN: 978-1-909132-34-4, Pages: 144,
Format: Paperback, Published: 2015
Also available in eBook format!

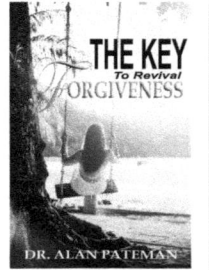

Forgiveness, The Key to Revival

Scripture is absolute when it comes to forgiveness. IF we forgive, THEN we are forgiven. It's that simple but no one said it was easy! Nonetheless, forgiveness can be likened to a spiritual key that unlocks spiritual doors and opportunities!

ISBN: 978-1-909132-41-2, Pages: 124,
Format: Paperback, Published: 2013
Also available in eBook format!

Apostles: Can the Church Survive Without Them?

Before Jesus returns a significant increase of the anointing will be poured out on the Body of Christ, but can the Church handle such an anointing? *(Acts 5:5)* Billy Brim once said, "As much as the anointing is powerful to create, it is as powerfully destructive of evil." The fear of God will be restored with the apostolic and people will begin walking with such anointing, as we have never seen before!

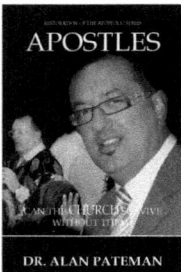

ISBN: 978-1-909132-04-7, Pages: 164,
Format: Paperback, Published: 2012
Also available in eBook format!

Dear Friends,

Have you considered becoming one of our international students? We are privileged to welcome you, from around the world, to "LifeStyle International Christian University" *(the teaching arm of Alan Pateman Ministries International)*. **An English speaking university** dedicated to your success; to see you trained and equipped to fully succeed in your God given Destiny.

It is our passion to raise up the leaders of tomorrow, who will have influence in all realms of authority, including the Body of Christ. Men and women of strategy, wisdom and true godliness, who'll stand with stature and maturity in this hour.

It's undeniable that in today's world, recognised education has become indispensable, therefore it is our desire to offer well balanced and well structured courses. Those that have been written by gifted and talented ministers of God, who seek to be inspired by God's Holy Spirit.

Consequently we have put together a **flexible curriculum,** designed both for correspondence students and campuses, which is a strategy to reach the distant learner; whether provincial, national or international. In fact we have many correspondence students from around the world, including a growing number of successful campuses, in various countries.

This is a growing platform, where men and women of dignity and passion, can grow and be established in their God given endeavours. As God is the healer of the nations, we pray and believe that many of our alumni will go on to **become world changers** in their own right.

We are proud of each and every one of our LICU students.
It would be our pleasure if you would join them on this incredible journey!

Doctor Alan Pateman

Alan Pateman Prof. Ph.D., D.Min., D.D., M.A., B.Th.
PRESIDENT AND CEO
www.licuuniversity.com www.cfeapostolicnetwork.com
Email: info@licuuniversity.com Mob: +39 366 329 1315

For more information visit our website/facebook or contact our office, using the details below:

Website: www.licuuniversity.com
Facebook: www.facebook.com/LICUMainCampus
Email: info@licuuniversity.com
Telephone: +39 366 329 1315

All Books Available

at

APMI PUBLICATIONS

Email: publications@alanpateman.com
*Also Available from Amazon.com
and other retail outlets.*

*If you purchased this book through Amazon.com
or other and enjoyed reading it, or perhaps one of
my other books, I would be grateful if you could
take a couple of minutes to write a Customer
Review, many thanks.*